T0282118

ELEPHANTS

ELEPHANTS

TOM JACKSON

amber
BOOKS

This pocket edition first published in 2024

First published in a hardback edition in 2020

Copyright © 2024 Amber Books Ltd

Published by
Amber Books Ltd
United House
London N7 9DP
United Kingdom

www.amberbooks.co.uk
Instagram: amberbooksltd
Pinterest: amberbooksltd
Twitter: @amberbooks

ISBN: 978-1-83886-359-3

Project Editor: Anna Brownbridge
Designer: Keren Harragan and Andrew Easton
Picture Research: Terry Forshaw

Printed in China

Contents

Introduction

O f the nine million species that share Planet Earth with us, the elephants are as close to our equals as any animal gets. Their immense size, huge ears, impressive tusks and outlandish trunk are what makes these giant beasts stick in the mind, but it is not what elevates them to their special place in our hearts. Anyone who has stood eye to eye

with an elephant will have marvelled at the immense creature and wondered what it makes of us. Looking closer, we find that elephants are not brutish grazers but intelligent animals that live a family life. We see a lot of our own society in the life of an elephant – from helpless calves to wise old matriarchs – and we might also see hints of a better way of living. Elephants are built for what life has to offer: a poor-quality diet of grass and leaves, a daily search for water and constant vigilance against parasites and predators. Elephants also face the threat of trophy hunters and poachers. Because of us, the future of these noble giants remains uncertain.

ABOVE:
A pair of tuskers joust. Elephants live in close-knit families where members are frequently testing out who is in charge.

OPPOSITE:
The anatomy of the African elephant is a consequence of many factors including low-quality food, tropical climate, predatory threats and the legacy of evolution.

Elephant Family

In the main, an elephant's life is spent with family. What looks to us at first glance like a herd of elephants – akin to a loose collection of animals, as we might see in deer, antelopes or cattle – is in fact a complete family unit, knitted together with strong bonds. The elephant family has around 25 members. The adult members – generally about 12 years and older – are all female. These bands of cow elephants are all under the auspices of the oldest female, a matriarch who is mostly their mother, aunt, or in some cases, older sister, first cousin or even grandmother. Meanwhile the adult males, or bulls, live a life apart, either alone or in a small band. (The matriarch drives them out of the family for good when the bulls approach maturity.) With a natural lifespan of 70 years or more, it takes decades for a matriarch to grow into her role. She knows when to keeping moving, when to stand ground, and where to find food and water during the tough times. When she dies, the next oldest family member will be well placed to take over. However, the matriarch is the first target in an ivory poaching attack – other elephants will not leave without her, making for easier kills. If the chief is killed young, there will be no obvious successor with the dominance and knowledge to take over, so the family fragments. It takes years for the wounds in elephant society to heal.

OPPOSITE:
Family life
The matriarch and other adult females will look after the younger elephants in the herd until they are about nine years old. At this age the elephants are approaching full size. The males then leave home, while the females begin to take on the work of the adults.

Extended family

Elephants in the wild, such as these African elephants, exhibit the behaviour of alloparenting, where a younger family member, generally a close relative, will take on the role of parent for a baby in place of the true parent. In the case of elephants, this is the way an allomother will learn how to care for her own young when the time comes.

PREVIOUS PAGES:
Asian species
The Asian elephant species has some obvious differences with the African one, most obviously the smaller ears. However, they also have low shoulders, with an obviously upward curving back.

OPPOSITE:
Gooey secretions
This female is exuding a thick secretion from glands on her temple. She does this when excited such as when a baby elephant is born in the group or during the breeding season. Males produce the smelly goo during the breeding season, known as musth, and it is a signal that the male is looking for mates and can be very aggressive towards other elephants.

BELOW:
Big hugs
Elephants are extremely tactile with other members of the family. The thick skin is nevertheless loaded with nerve endings and so is highly sensitive to all kinds of physical contact.

Mother knows best

The family does everything together. It eats together and moves together and it is the matriarch who decides when and where to go, and always leads the way. Her venerable age means she has lived through most scenarios: drought, wildfire, flood and attacks from lions, leopards and hyenas, so she already knows what to do – and what not to do. There is some truth to the saying 'Elephants never forget'.

17

ABOVE:

Life-long care
Once fully mature at about 12 years old, a female elephant can give birth every three or four years. However, most take longer than this and have about four calves in their lifetimes and can theoretically become pregnant at any age, although births after the age of 50 are rare.

OPPOSITE TOP:

Tapped up
Every member of the family makes time to stay on friendly terms with every other member. This can take a lot of time so, if all else is well, family members simply tap hello with their trunks.

OPPOSITE BOTTOM:

Stays close
For the first few years of a calf's life he or she will be kept on a short leash – or a short trunk – and is seldom allowed to stray more than a trunk's length from the mother or other adult female.

African species

The African elephant diverged from the ancestors
of the Asian elephant about two million years ago.
It has a pronounced ridge at the shoulder blades,
which provides anchorage for the muscles holding up
the massive head. This ridge is not seen in the Asian
species, which has a convex back.

Water supply

A family of elephants needs to drink regularly and is never more than a day's walk from a watering hole. Instead of lowering its head to drink, it sucks up water with the trunk and squirts it into the mouth. However, it does not drink through the trunk, which is one popular misconception.

Learning to do

African elephants become adults at the age of about 12 years, while Asian elephants reach maturity at 14 years. As well as growing the body, the years of development also involve learning from the mother about how to find food and water and how to interact with other elephants.

LEFT:

Big ears

As well as the obvious role in providing hearing, the elephant's ears, or specifically the outer ear, has three other functions. To radiate away excess heat, to swat flies, and to send signals to other elephants and nearby creatures.

ABOVE:

Littlest elephants

The forest elephants of Borneo are a subspecies of the Asian elephant. Members of this isolated population of elephants are only marginally smaller than elephants on the Asian mainland, but they have large ears and longer tails.

Stick together

A band of African elephants heads to a watering hole. The gang members all have their ears spread wide, perhaps to ward off a swarm of bugs – a quick bath will help with that – or as a warning signal to other animals to keep their distance. The message is clear: Animals with ears this big should not be messed with.

Subspecies

The Asian elephant is divided into four main populations. The mainland groups are often called Indian elephants despite also living in the Himalayan countries and across Southeast Asia. Sri Lanka is home to a large population; two smaller ones also live on Sumatra and in the forests of Borneo – mostly the Malaysian sector.

Wild islanders

Most Asian elephants live in captivity, but these Borneo elephants are one of the most significant wild populations. Tradition dictates that the pygmy elephants are the descendants of a herd imported in the 17th century but, DNA evidence shows the elephants have been on the island for 300,000 years.

BELOW:
Cooling spray

A mother sprays some water from her highly adaptable trunk on to her calf – and herself. The purpose of this is to cool off – although cleaning is also a benefit. A large animal like an elephant sheds body heat only slowly, especially in humid jungle conditions, and so a quick shower is a great relief.

OPPOSITE TOP:
Group bath

Waterholes are choke points, and ideal places for a predator to find a steady stream of prey who cannot avoid visiting the area. Elephants are safer than most, but they are protective of calves and so the whole family takes a bath together.

OPPOSITE BOTTOM:
Muddy waters

The elephants are not fussed about the cleanliness of the water. In fact they like a bit of mud and silt which is healthy for their surprisingly sensitive skin – requiring of a lot of attention.

Curled up

Compared to overall body size, the Asian elephant has a longer trunk than the African species, so much so that it would drag on the ground if it were not habitually rolled up at the tip, when not being used.

Hidden from danger
A calf that is only a few days old is given close protection by its elders. They keep it hidden from view by mingling the little one with their trunks and legs.

Play time
The younger members of the family spend a long time playing. Games involve general rough and tumble and trunk tangles and tussles. The young ones are learning how to form bonds with each other through tactile and visual signals, and the limits of acceptable behaviours.

Protection
Despite being destined to grow into the largest land animal on Earth, an elephant calf is an easy kill for Africa's bug hunters. The mother is not taking any chances with this precious member of the family and has all angles covered, even a sneaky aerial attack from a leopard leaping down from a tree.

ABOVE:
Nuclear family
A cow elephant seldom gives birth to more than one calf at a time. Nevertheless, it would not be uncommon to raise two children at once. By the time a third is born, the oldest offspring will be more or less independent.

OPPOSITE TOP:
Head to tail
Elephant families often move in single file. The younger members firmly grab hold of the tail of the elephant in front with their trunks. This helps to pull them along and ensures the column of elephants stays close together.

OPPOSITE BOTTOM:
Smaller groups
In dryer habitats, such as the African grasslands, families frequently split up into smaller groups of mother and calves who forage for whatever food they can find.

Active at night

An elephant has little time for anything other than looking for food, eating it and then searching for more. It will spend 16 hours a day doing this, and is frequently active late into the night.

Take on water

A large elephant will drink 170 litres (45 gallons) of water every day. This vast amount equates to more than the entire volume of a standard sized bathtub.

Looking for danger

Living out in the open savannah means that predators can approach from any direction but they will struggle to stay hidden from detection. The mother elephant is always on the lookout for danger – and more importantly listening and smelling for threats.

Elder leads
This elephant family has formed up into a defensive formation with the smallest and most vulnerable animals tucked safely between the older and stronger members. The oldest and toughest of them all is out front facing dangers head on.

OPPOSITE:
Tusks growth
The tusks are growing from the elephant's upper jaw from birth. This mother
African elephant has had her tusks sawn away by park rangers to stop her and her
family being targeted by poachers. Nevertheless, they are steadily growing back.

ABOVE:
Mouth to mouth
A peckish calf reaches in to its doting mother's mouth and snaffles a bit of well-
chewed food. This is the way calves eat solid foods until they are around four
years old.

Seeking shade

In the heat of the midday sun, these African elephants are keeping cool in a pool of shade. Larger animals shed heat more slowly than smaller ones due to a bigger mass-to-volume ratio. Without taking steps to keep cool, African elephants would become dangerously overheated.

ABOVE:
Sniff danger
It might look like this
family of African
elephants is waving
a cheery hello to the
photographer. However,
they are nervously
sniffing the air with
their trunks for signs
of danger.

OPPOSITE:
Water carrier
Elephants are rarely
more than 25km (15
miles) from a source of
water, which is roughly
the distance the family
are able to walk in
one day.

PREVIOUS PAGES:
Thunderstruck
Elephants can hear the deep rumble of thunder from 280km (175 miles) away. They will head towards the sound – and vibrations running through the ground – in the hope of finding a supply of fresh water.

LEFT:
No jumping
These playing calves are testing out the limits of their bodies. They will find that the elephants are the only animals that are unable to jump, even when still young and relatively small. The sturdy skeleton is built to carry the animal's immense weight but that prevents it from jumping on all four feet at once.

OPPOSITE:
Dust jacket
Both mother and child are smothered in the red dust of the African savannah. The dust acts as an insect repellent warding off parasites such as warble flies which lay their eggs in the elephants' skin. The maggots that hatch eat their way through the host's skin before tunnelling out.

ABOVE:
Dominance
Despite the outward appearance of cooperation and caring, elephant families are based on a hierarchy which takes form in the earliest years. The play fights and trunk twists so beloved by calves set the scene for which of the sisters – and which of the brothers – will be chief one day.

Mud bath

As well as water, an elephant family visits a watering hole for its mud, and will have a good wallow in it to get a thick coating of grime. To the elephants the mud is not dirt but a pest resistant coating that oozes into every crack in the thick, rough hide. The mud will make it harder for jungle parasites, most obviously bloodsucking leeches and ticks, to latch on to the body.

OPPOSITE:
Crossing a river
Elephants are good
swimmers but this
mother and sister are not
taking any chances with
the latest addition to an
Asian elephant family
as they cross a river
in Pinnawela elephant
orphanage, Sri Lanka.

BELOW:
Attack alert
As a family of African
elephants crosses a
track the matriarch
signals a warning to
an approaching threat,
giving the smaller and
less experienced family
members time to shift to
a safer location.

PREVIOUS PAGES:
Shorter tusks
Due to the pressure of poaching, where families with large tusks are killed to supply the illegal ivory market, the average length of an African elephant's tusks has halved in the last century.

ABOVE:
Practice battle
A little tussle between younger family members keeps them calm and reduces restlessness in the wider group – and one day it might be played out for real in a musth-fuelled battle for mates.

RIGHT:
Strong bonds
The bond between mother and calf is constantly being reinforced by little touches of the trunk, rumbling calls and eye contact. Here a very little calf tries to wrap its trunk around its mother's trunk akin to a human toddler's hand only able to grip one of its parent's fingers.

Calming presence
An elephant family has a common emotional state, with members taking their cues from each other. Just as one elephant can rapidly spread alarm through the group, it can also calm down the other elephants with a series of tactile and visual signals and sounds.

Elephant Body

An elephant is unmistakeable thanks to its unique anatomical features. Add to that the fact that the African elephant is the largest land animal on Earth, with bulls growing 7.5m (24.5ft) long and standing 3.3m (10.8ft) tall. At 6.4m (21ft) long and 3m (10ft) high, the Asian elephant is smaller but comes in at an easy second place.

The Asian elephant exists in several isolated populations (although very few are living wild) which are treated as three or four subspecies. Some authorities prefer to divide the African species into two distinct species, with the giant tuskers of the savannah known as bush elephants, while its habitually smaller relatives from the forests of Central and West Africa (seldom more than 2.8m [9.2ft] tall) are called the African forest elephants. The fragmentation of habitats over the centuries has meant the two types of elephant seldom meet and have thus evolved significant genetic differences. Nevertheless, some biologists still regard the groups as two subspecies.

All elephants evolved from large swamp creatures that used long spade-shaped tusks to dig for food. Today, the lower tusks have been lost, and the upper lip and nose have evolved into the famous trunk.

OPPOSITE:
Three body features
The trio of trunk, tusk and
giant outer ear is a unique anatomical feature of the
elephant. All of them carry out various functions
to do with feeding, the senses, protection and
communication, and together they are the best way
to identify one species from the other.

PREVIOUS PAGES:
Skull

Elephants have a vast skull. This is not just to hold its heavy brain, weighing 5.4kg (12lb). The human brain is only 1.6kg (3.5lb). If anything there is too much space in the head, which is created by the immense facial bones that are used to hold the tusks and trunk. As a result, the elephant skull is filled with sinus (air spaces) and foramina (holes), which cut down on weight.

LEFT:
Tusk

The elephant tusk is a long upper incisor which grows out through the upper lip. The tusk is a tooth but also famously made of ivory. This material is mostly made from dentine, which is the softer interior of the tooth and which is strengthened with extra calcium. These is also a thin outer layer of enamel.

OPPOSITE:
Mouth
The facial anatomy of an elephant is so unusual that it is easy to be confused by it. The trunk is an extension of the nose and not the mouth, which is hidden underneath it for most of the time.

ABOVE:
Fifth limb
The trunk is like the elephant's fifth – and most agile – limb. It can be used as hands to pick up food, such as this tasty bunch of greens. The entire structure is able to contort in all directions thanks to 100,000 separate muscle blocks.

Wet play
While frequent bathing is essential to keep the elephants rugged skin healthy and moisturized, elephants young and old do not pass up the opportunity for a bit of fun.

BELOW:
Look, no tusks
While both male and female African elephants grow
tusks, female Asian elephants generally do not. This
species difference has been something of a curse for
the African elephant, where entire families are being
targeted by the illegal ivory trade, whereas in Asia,
only the solitary bulls are hunted.

RIGHT:
Sensitive touch
Although it is easily powerful enough to send a person
flying with a single well-aimed blow, the trunk is also
capable of very fine movements, such as those needed
to rub some mud out of the eye.

Ear shapes

Elephant experts learn to identify individuals from the shapes of the ears, which have uniquely ragged edges and networks of veins. It is uncertain if elephants use these cues to identify friends but they are good at remembering who's who, and can even recognize themselves in a mirror.

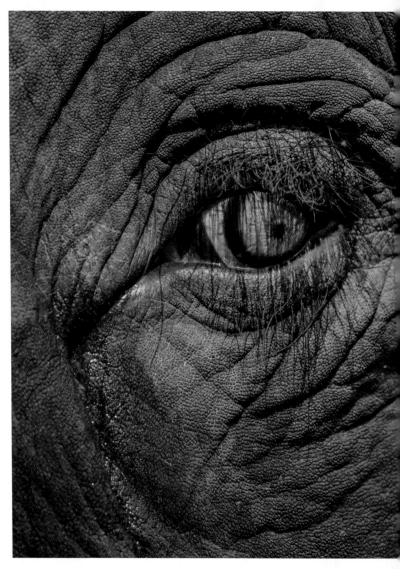

Vision

One thing about an elephant that is small is its eye. Elephant vision is poor. The animal can see clearly for about 10m (33ft) and can make out objects double that distance away but after that it relies on hearing and smell to detect food, water and threats.

Master tusk

It is common for an elephant to favour one tusk over the other and use it more often just as humans rely on the left or right hand. Tusks are seldom the same length and the so-called master tusk is frequently worn down a little due to its extra use.

OPPOSITE TOP:

One finger or two?

This tusk belongs to an African elephant. We know this because there are two fleshy protuberances, one above, the other below. These work like fingers to touch and grip when delicacy is required. An Asian elephant has but a single finger on the top edge of the trunk.

OPPOSITE BOTTOM:

Taste sensation

Contrary to what we learn from the way that animals are sometimes portrayed in cartoons and movies, elephants do not like sticky buns or any sweet foods. They prefer the taste of twigs, leaves and grass.

ABOVE:

Tail

The elephant's tail can grow to almost 2m (6.5ft). Normally, it is always on the move, swinging from side to side. When the elephant stiffens its tail and holds it still, this is a sign that the animal is anxious about something.

Hair and skin

Although it is hard to see on many elephants, due to their use of mud and dust to treat the skin, elephants are covered in coarse hairs. The hairs are not there to keep the animal warm but to protect it from bright sunlight.

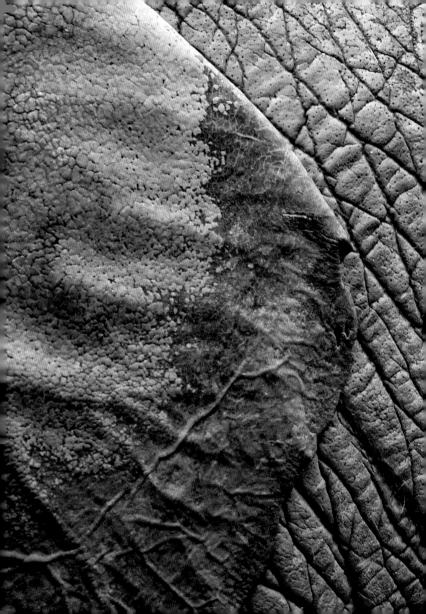

OPPOSITE:

No sweat

The thick skin of an elephant has no sweat pores. The quantity of water that would be required to actively cool a body of this size by the evaporation of sweat would be far too high to be practical. Instead heat is radiated away through the large surface area of the ears, which are fed with venous blood.

BELOW:

Listen up

As well as picking up sounds with the ears, elephants listen with the feet to detect the deep infrasonic vibrations – too deep for our ears to hear – travelling through the ground. To get a clearer signal, the animal lifts the unused foot clear of the ground.

PREVIOUS PAGES:
Age indicator
The tusks never stop growing and so their length can be a good indicator of an elephant's age. The largest tusks on record were 3.51m (11.5ft) long and weighed 117kg (258lb).

BELOW:
Smell
As well as being the biggest nose in the world, an elephant's trunk is also one of the most sensitive sniffers in the animal kingdom. The long nose can sniff out water from nearly 20km (12 miles) away.

OPPOSITE:
Forehead
Another identifying difference between elephant species is the forehead. Asian elephants have a giveaway cleft in the forehead, while their African cousins have a rounded head.

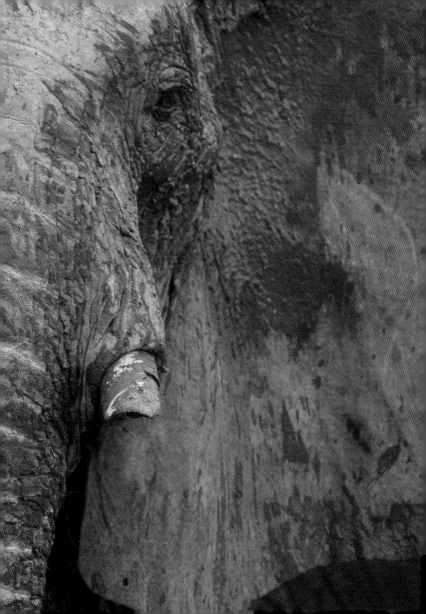

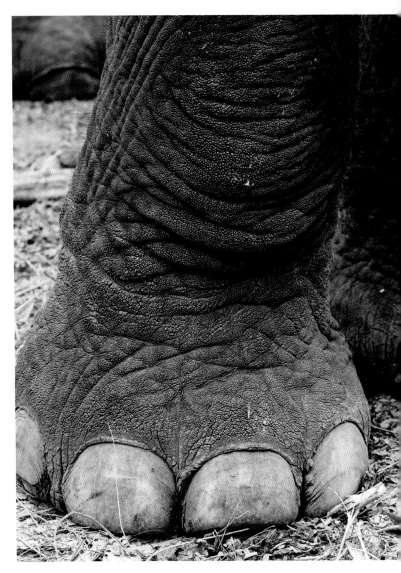

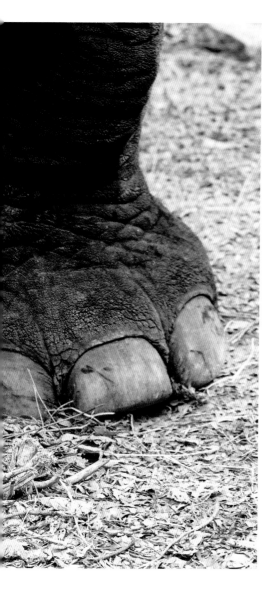

PREVIOUS PAGES:

Sun screen

This alarming adult elephant has coated itself in the soft red dust of the Kenyan savannah, baked dry by the summer heat. The dust will act as a sun screen, protecting the big elephant during the long hours exposed to the baking equatorial sunshine.

LEFT:

Toe nails

Elephants walk on the tips of their toes, in much the same way that a horse, hippo, or goat does. The hooves of these animals are their equivalent of toenails, which support and protect the bony digits. Flat-footed elephants retain individual toe nails which are continually worn down as the animal walks. The Asian elephant (seen here) has five on the front feet and four on the back.

ABOVE:
Heel
There is no bone in the elephant's heel, instead the toe bones at the front of the foot are surrounded by a fatty pad, which absorbs the great weight of the animal.

OPPOSITE:
Heavyweight
An African bull elephant weighs 6 tonnes – twice the weight of the female. Male Asian elephants are only marginally more light on their feet at 5.4 tonnes (which is about the same weight as the tongue of a blue whale!).

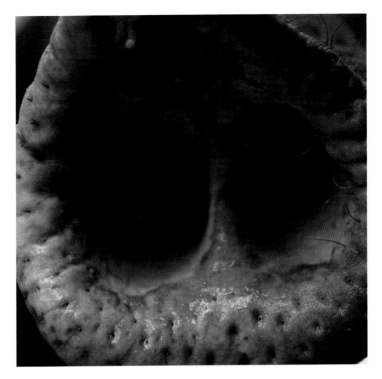

Dark skinned

The skin of elephants often appears paler, even red or yellow, due to the application of dust and mud. However, underneath it all the skin is naturally dark grey, almost black in Asian animals, which also often have pink and peach spots on the forehead and trunk.

OPPOSITE:
Skin

Up to 4cm (1.8in) thick in places and the elephant's hide will become cracked if left to dry out for long periods, and those cracks are easily infested by bacteria and parasites.

RIGHT TOP:
Nostril

The nostrils run all the way down the trunk, so there are two continuous tubes running the entire length divided by a cartilage barrier called the septum.

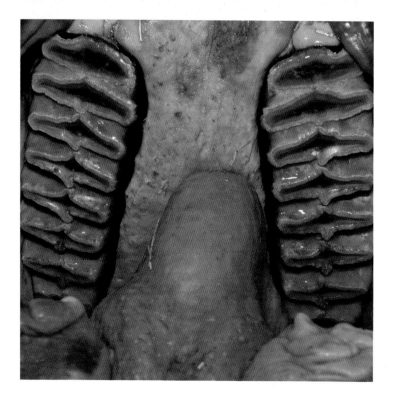

Four teeth

Ignoring the tusks, which are technically teeth, the elephant has four teeth inside its mouth. The long molars are very rough and used to crush and grind wood and leaves into a pulp. As it is used and worn down the tooth moves forward in the mouth until its falls out – and is replaced with another. Its lifetime supply is 24 teeth.

OPPOSITE:

Look, no bones

There are no bones inside the trunk. Its strength and manoeuvrability are due to the fluid inside being contained under pressure. The trunk as a whole, and the many segments within it, can change shape but not volume and so it resists the push and pull of the muscles and that contorts it into different positions.

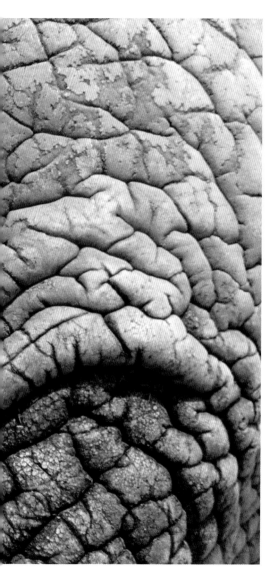

Gas production
Elephants ferment their food and that produces a lot of methane gas. It is estimated that an elephant farts and burps out enough methane each day to fuel a 32-km (20-mile) car journey.

Elephant Behaviour

The sight of an elephant in the wild is awe-inspiring. As we watch it move with such power and grace and pause to feed or drink using its dexterous trunk, we are quickly drawn in to wanting to understand how an elephant lives, how it survives, and what drives its complex behaviours. Ethologists, the scientists who study animal behaviour and analyse its purpose, have studied all species of elephant in the wild and in captivity. They watch how the great animals interact with each other from birth to death, and figure out why they do it this way. They have learnt that not only does it take a long time for an elephant to grow into a full sized adult – around 10 to 14 years, it also takes just as long – perhaps longer – for a young elephant to learn how to behave like an elephant.

The apparent serenity of elephant life is maintained by an uneasy balance between mutual self-interest and the threat of extreme violence. The adult females need to work together to raise their young, and gang together in family groups. There is little that can upset the harmony within the family, where elephants work hard to maintain good relations. The main disruptors are the males, who are cast out for much of the year but drawn into the family during the breeding seasons, bringing with them rivalries that are played out in battle.

OPPOSITE:

Rogue male

A lone African elephant is most certainly a male. He was pushed out of the family by the matriarch as he approached maturity, and may have joined a small group of other expelled males. Today he prefers to live alone, and seldom tolerates company of any kind for very long.

Trunk call
Dexterous handler, sensitive nose, tender feeler, visual aid, water mover, lethal weapon... what else can a trunk do? Well it can also be used as a snorkel when the elephant opts to lie on its side in shallow water.

OPPOSITE:
Reach for it

The trunk is useful for reaching up to get hold of the most succulent leaves that grow out of reach of most savannah animals. The elephant's pillar-like legs are built to carry the animal's extreme weight and are not well suited to agility. However, the animal can support its weight on its back legs for a short time.

BELOW:
Trumpet

The sound of an elephants trumpet is one of the most recognizable animals calls – albeit one that is hard to emulate. Hearing a trumpet signals that the elephant is very exercised about something, perhaps lost, angry, or surprised. The trumpet is produced by pushing air through the trunk not the larynx.

Wetland home
The permanent waters
of Botswana's Okavango
Delta is home to one
sixth of the world's
elephant population.
Here a solitary elephant
reaps a meal of grasses
in a flooded meadow.

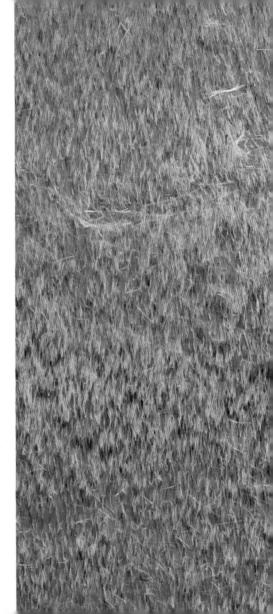

LEFT:
Calling card
The trumpet sound of
an elephant is a blend of
harmonic and discordant
tomes. African elephants
are able to identify
a family member from
the sound of their call
alone from 2.5km
(1.5 miles) away.

ABOVE:
Evolutionary route
One suggested theory
for the evolution of the
elephant's trunk is that
it evolved as a snorkel
(with benefits) as the
ancestors of today's
elephants were swamp
feeders, digging for food
in shallow water.

Move together
This African elephant family is on the move. Elephants seldom stay in one place for more than about 15 minutes before the matriarch decides to lead her family to the next feeding spot. Out on the savannah the group could move 25 km (15 miles) each day. For forest elephants where food is plentiful, progress is generally slow in a forest habitat and the family only covers a few kilometres a day.

Ocean encounter

Elephants are not spooked by the ocean and will take a dip in the surf when they reach the coast. There are frequent reports of elephants being spotted far out at sea – often too far to get back to shore.

Alone time

Older bull elephants tend to live alone. This giant tusker will have made many enemies over the years as he battled with rivals each breeding season. Built to fight, and packing twice the weight of a female elephant, it is best to stay away, especially during the musth season when the males are literally driven wild by the calls of the females.

BELOW:
Mud pack

Mud has a medicinal function for the elephant. This young one is making sure it is thoroughly covered in this cooling emollient – and it looks like they are helping another family member as well.

Ocean voyage
It is rare for elephants to get out of their depth apart from in the sea. They float low in the water but raising a snorkel ensures they do not drown, and they are strong swimmers using the flat feet as paddles.

Megaherbivore

Forest elephants are browsers, which means they pluck leaves from trees and bushes, while out on the savannah they survive as grazers, wrenching out mouthfuls of grass with a twist of the trunk. The Asian elephant alone has been recorded eating 112 different kinds of plant foods.

BELOW:
Danger

Each year around 500 people are killed by African elephants – none of whom are truly tamed. The number of deaths from Asian elephants is higher due to the animals being worked as beasts of burden. Most deaths are from attacks by males during the breeding season.

ABOVE:

Trunk twist

The dividing line between a playful greeting and an
all-out attack is a fine one. Here a pair of Sri Lankan
elephants are saying hello by entwining their trunks.
Rival males will do much the same thing but also bring
their tusks to bear as they test each other's strength.

RIGHT:

Charge!

As well as matching the weight of a small truck, this
charging matriarch can match its acceleration and hits
a speed of 40km/h (25mph) in a few seconds. Most
charges are shams meant to scare off threats, but
do not wait to find out.

Finding water

During the dry season, every family member is focused on finding water. They listen for the rumbles of thunder, search for dark clouds, and seek out the whiff of water.

Raised near water

Many Asian elephants are born into captivity and trained as domestic animals. It is common for elephant farms to be located next to a river to make life more comfortable for the elephants.

Always eating

Elephants require an enormous amount of food, so they are always eating. On average an adult elephant will chow down on 280kg (620lb) of plant food. That is two-thirds the weight of a horse.

Well-trodden paths
Elephants frequently
follow the same routes
through their territories.
The matriarch who leads
the way will have learnt
them from her mother or
grandmother. Elephant
brains have highly
convoluted temporal
lobes. It is suggested that
this is where the animals
store a lifetime of
memories about where
to go and when.

LEFT:
Sharing the plains
Elephants are the biggest
African animals, but
by no means the most
numerous. Antelopes of
all sizes form vast herds
that coexist around
the elephants.

OPPOSITE TOP:
Man to man
A bull elephant makes
an impressive figure,
but the male lion thinks
that he is the ruler of
the savannah. This
stand-off was seen in the
Serengeti National Park,
Tanzania.

OPPOSITE BOTTOM:
Breeding rivals
Males tolerate each
other, but when drawn to
receptive females during
the breeding season they
cannot avoid conflict.
Fights involve charging
head on and gouging
with tusks.

ABOVE:
Quick snooze
Elephants don't require
as many hours of sleep
as humans do, they
snatch a total of just
four or five hours sleep
a day, often while
standing up or while
leaning against a tree.

Constant search

An elephant's life is a relentless search for food which takes up three-quarters of their time. They need a near-constant and large supply of their low-quality plant foods. A large body is more efficient to run than a smaller one and only something as vast as an elephant can survive on a diet of twigs, bark, leaves and grass.

BELOW:
Sharpen up
African elephants will keep their tusks sharp and filed by rubbing them against a branch or a tree trunk. They use their tusks for digging, ripping bark of trees, foraging, carrying heavy objects and for resting a heavy trunk on.

OPPOSITE TOP:
Tough foods
In hard times, elephants will shift from eating leaves and grass to bark, twigs and even crunch up wood. All its food is digested with the help of stomach bacteria. These microbes are able to break down cellulose, the main constituent of plant food. It is unaffected by animal stomach enzymes.

OPPOSITE BOTTOM:
Heavy lifter
The elephant's great strength and powerful trunk allows it to access food that is beyond the reach of other herbivores. This one is pushing over a tree to reach its leaves. If unable to move on frequently to find fresh foods, a herd of elephants will readily denude an area of trees – and then starve to death.

Four knees

Elephants are the only animals on Earth to have four knees, or limb joints that bend forward (elbows go backwards). This arrangement is there to ensure the elephants axillary skeleton (the limbs and other peripheral structures) is robust enough to support the animal's weight.

Queen of the plains

A pride of lions offers a real and present danger to a young elephant calf. During the day lions like to lounge in the shade, resting up before slipping into the night to wreak havoc. This elephant matriarch is not prepared to give them that chance and launches a daytime raid to chase the predators away.

LEFT:

Migration

The Okavango Delta is not a river mouth as its name suggests. It is far from the ocean and forms instead an inland depression that is fed by a series of rivers. When the rest of southern Africa is drying out, the Delta brims with water, and thousands of African elephants migrate here to feast on its bounty.

BELOW:

Wet look

A love of water comes with a downside for elephants. Billions of insect larvae, often bloodsucking flies, live in the muddy pools. Mud is the first line of defence against these pesky pests.

PREVIOUS PAGES:
Bigger groups
In the wet season, the
African elephant forms
back into their full-scale
family, or even gather
as a multi-family clan,
as they migrate to areas
where there is plenty
of food.

LEFT:
Tolerance
In times of plenty, the
elephant family is a
model of harmony.
However, as soon as the
food and water begins to
run out the wider group
will begin to fragment,
as younger mothers and
calves opt to try their
chances away from their
leader. The division
is temporary, with
subgroups keeping tabs
on each other's locations.

PREVIOUS PAGES:
Asian wanderer
An Asian elephant family lives a nomadic life moving frequently through a forest home range of about 600sq km (230sq miles). This family is in Sri Lanka.

LEFT:
Salts
Elephants need salts which are often lacking from their plant foods. Water, the muddier the better, may contain these minerals. In the Mount Elgon National Park in Kenya, elephants have been seen digging salty clays from underground caves with their tusks. They feel their way around in the dark with their trunks.

157

OPPOSITE:
Half digested
Less than 50 per cent of the nutrients in an elephant's
meal are extracted by the gut. Elephant faeces are
a useful food source of other animals.

ABOVE:
Deep sleep
Most of an elephant's sleep is a light doze but they
must have a deep sleep from time to time. To do that
the elephant must lie down, which they only manage
for a couple of hours at a time every three or four days.

Feeling the way
When uncertain about which way to go in an unfamiliar place, the elephant will prod the ground in front of it with its trunk to check it can hold its weight. Only once it has tested the way ahead will it proceed.

Bachelor party
After being made to leave their family, bull elephants often gather in smaller all-male herds. The social bonds in these groups are much weaker than in the female-led families.

Sri Lankan elephants

The Asian elephants living on the island of Sri Lanka tend to be larger than animals from the mainland and Indonesia. Another defining difference is that few of the Sri Lankan elephants are growing tusks. There are no female tuskers and only about seven per cent of the males grow them.

OPPOSITE:
A trunkful
An adult elephant's trunk has many exceptional features, one of these being that it can hold about 6 litres (1.3 gallons) of water – and squirt it too.

BELOW:
Working day
A large number of Asian elephants live in captivity. They are traditionally used to shift logs in remote jungle building sites, where working vehicles cannot reach.

Earth movers

The land frequented by elephants, such as this muddy watering hole in Addo National Elephant Park, South Africa, is rapidly denuded of vegetation, as the visitors uproot the trees nearby and eat every last twig.

OVERLEAF:

Orphanage

As social animals, captive elephants are raised in conditions as close to natural ones as possible. These orphan Asian elephants are fostered with unrelated elephants in an ad hoc family which will give them more of a chance of living a normal adult life.

BELOW:
Bottom first
Elephants seldom lie
down, but when they do
they hit the ground with
their rear end first. The
process of sitting down
is slow, but standing
back up again is even
slower Manoeuvring this
giant frame takes a lot
of time and effort.

OPPOSITE:
Falling numbers
The wild populations
of elephants are at
near historical lows
worldwide. In Asia,
50,000 elephants live in
the wild and appear to
be in decline. The wild
population of African
elephants is 30,000.
In recent years, after
decades of decline, this
number has started to
rise again.

Elephant Tales
Local people believe that old elephants climb Mount Kilimanjaro, a tall volcano in East Africa, and throw themselves into a hidden crater to die. This and other stories of elephant graveyards are just legends.

TOP:
Seeds
The plant foods that are eaten by the elephants rely on these great beasts to distribute seeds. The seeds pass untouched through the elephant's gut – or are prepared to germinate by stomach acids – and are deposited far from the parent plant in a steaming heap of natural fertilizer.

RIGHT:
Tusk muscles
The tusk is moved using 16 major muscles located at the top and side. These produce the large scale movements, raising the tusk upward and from side to side. Smaller muscles are used for finer movements.

Good neighbours
The needs of an elephant, such as this lonesome male, seldom conflict with those of other plain dwellers, but most other animals, including these impala, keep their distance.

PREVIOUS PAGES:
Rough and ready
The wrinkled skin
of this bull may look
damaged and in need of
care but the deep fissures
help to trap water and
keep the skin damp and
moisturised long after
the elephant has finished
his bath.

OPPOSITE:
Home range
The size of an African
elephant's home range
depends on its habitat.
In the lush grasslands
of Tanzania, the family
occupies just 10sq km
(4sq miles), but in the
arid semi-desert of
Namibia that territory
is 18,000sq km
(7000sq miles).

RIGHT:
Dig for survival
When there is no water
left in pools and rivers,
elephants will start
to dig into the muddy
banks, using the tusks
to excavate down to the
water table – often with
limited success.

Feathered friend

A cattle egret is hitching a ride on the back of an elephant calf. Normally the long-legged bird will follow behind a herd of elephants, snapping up any insects and other little creatures that are disturbed by the giant beasts lumbering overhead.

Streaking

As night falls, a family of elephants begin a streak. They pick up speed – although only to about 4km/h (2.5mph) and move in a straight line through their home territory. Streaking is a mysterious activity. It generally occurs on well-trodden paths and it may be a way that the matriarch gets her family across territory that has proven dangerous in the past.

Elephant Calves

As the rains arrive, love is in the air for the world's elephants. With a gestation period of almost two years, a successful mating in the rainy season will ensure the calf will be born at the same time of year, and that means the mother will have plenty of water to provide the milk for her newborn. Both Asian and African elephants are capable of producing young at any time of the year and, intelligent as they are, elephant parents do not confer on family planning. However, a mother will not be receptive to mating for a further two or three years after giving birth, and in this way the breeding episodes have become synchronized to the local rain.

When born each calf is welcomed into the family. In other social animals, from deer to lions, mothers frequently withdraw from the group to give birth in private, and then introduce the new arrival with some caution to the wider group. Nothing could be further from the truth with elephants, where one or two sisters or cousins will attend the birth as midwives, and as soon as the calf is out, the entire family comes to tap hello with the trunks, so they can learn the scent of the latest member, and he or she can learn theirs. The elephant breeding strategy seems to work because 95 per cent of calves survive into adolescence, a success rate almost unheard of in wild animals.

OPPOSITE:
Long childhood
There is no need for this calf to hurry.
It will take at least 12 years to reach an
adult size and will still be learning from
its elders until the age of 17.

Touch

The sense of touch is very important to an elephant calf. It starts using its trunk to explore its surroundings – and its playmates – straight from birth. Calves have been known to suck their own trunk like newborn babies might use their thumb.

Eye open

Elephant calves are born with their eyes open. They are only about 1m (3ft) tall at birth – but they will grow quickly, at about 2–3cm (0.8–1.2in) per month.

First walk

Elephant calves are relatively precocious and able to stand from about the age of 30 minutes and are walking within the hour – not too fast though!

PREVIOUS PAGES:
Suckle

Cow elephants have two mammary glands located between the front legs. The calve sucks with its mouth, not its trunk as some might expect. The calf will drink only milk for three months and then it will begin to experiment with solid foods.

RIGHT:
Weight

An African elephant weighs 120kg (265lb) at birth. It will put on 500g a day in the first few weeks of life. Elephant calves stay close to their mother, but this one has temporarily left the safety of her side.

OPPOSITE:
Multiple births
Twin elephants are very rare with less than one birth in 100 producing more than one calf. However, the mother should be able to raise both her calves given favourable conditions.

BELOW:
Learn by play
Like baby mammals across the animal kingdom, the elephant calf will learn how to look after itself through play and by copying the behaviour of the adults in the family that surrounds them.

BELOW:

Trunk control

It takes several months for the calf to learn to take full control of its trunk. There is a lot of trial and error as it builds the neural patterns to create smooth movements using the many hundreds of muscles involved.

RIGHT:

Unsteady on its feet

As it learns to take control of its massive body and use it in many settings, such as rolling in a mud bath, taking a swim, or ripping up grass from the ground, the little elephant will take a few tumbles.

PREVIOUS PAGES:
A long time coming

The gestation period – the length of a pregnancy – in African elephants is 22 months. The pregnancy might be a month or two shorter in Asian elephants because the babies are smaller, but both species have longer gestation periods than any other mammal. Even a blue whale is finished in 12 months!

BELOW:
Hairy young

All elephant calves, Asian ones especially, are born much hairier than the elders. This thick mop of hair on the head and back helps to ward off the worst effects of the heat of the sun.

OPPOSITE:
Weight

An Asian elephant weighs 100kg (220 lb) at birth. It will take slightly longer – 14 years – to reach full adult size than members of the African species.

Smell together
One of the first things a newborn calf does when it is strong enough is to smell its mother's dung. That distinctive whiff creates a special bond between mother and child. More widely the family has a group scent, and newborns are surrounded by the herd in a celebration of its birth. The females release a smelly musth and the baby to takes in the odours that identify its kin.

BELOW:
Wet season
This little African elephant has been enjoying a mud bath. This shows that it has been born at a time of year when water is plentiful, and the grass and other plants in the region will provide lush food for months ahead.

Play time
While the older
elephants work hard
to find food by pulling
down tree branches and
digging up tender roots,
the calf has plenty of
time to run and play.

OPPOSITE TOP:
Keeping up
When the herd goes on the move, the calves have to keep up. They are pulled along by their mother, who will not want to fall behind the main family group.

OPPOSITE BOTTOM:
Growing independence
At the age of around 12 years old, a calf will be expected to care entirely for itself but is still dependent on the matriarch. Males are driven out of the group by the big female around the age of 15, just before its female sisters and cousins become ready to have their first calves.

ABOVE:
Weaning
A calf begins to wean itself off milk by taking the pre-chewed foods out of the mouths of its mother and older siblings. This is one mechanism for introducing healthy stomach bacteria to the calf. Another is for the calf to eat small amounts of its mother's dung.

Protection

Although it weighs more than a grown adult man from day one, the older elephants protect the calf. A big cat or pack of hunting dogs would not hesitate if given the opportunity to kill it.

214

OPPOSITE:
Dependent
The safest place for the little calf is among the forest of tree-trunk legs of its mother and herd in general. There is no predator on Earth that will attempt to attack it there.

BELOW:
Raised in captivity
About a third of Asian elephants are born and raised in captivity, sadly to be used either as working animals or to be used in the tourism industry.

BELOW:

Feeding time

The cow elephant always suckles standing up, so the calf has to be standing also. The trunk is rolled back over one eye to get out of the way of the hungry mouth.

OPPOSITE TOP:

Chewing

The calf is born with its first four cheek teeth ready to erupt so it can start to chomp on the twigs and leaves that will sustain it for the next 70 years. Yum!

OPPOSITE BOTTOM:

Short rest

Being born is hard work. The midwives, or allomothers, help to clean off the baby as it arrives, and then it is given a short rest before being helped to its feet.

Safe and sound

The calf stays close to its mother, and all seems serene to us, but the little one is surrounded by a cacophony of infrasound coming from the herd.

The whiff of danger

A pair of playful calves pause their frolicks to sniff the air for a threat. They must always be aware of what is going on around them, even when they are having so much fun.

Drought risk

This calf seems to be full of energy as it charges through the dust, but if the drought conditions persist, its mother will not find the food she needs to make milk for her young. Starvation is a possibility.

Who goes there?

If it were not for the tall grasses giving it scale, this elephant might look just like a giant matriarch or bull approaching down a forest trail. The future is uncertain for this African bush elephant and all its cousins with threats from poaching, habitat loss and climate changes. But if anyone will tough it out, it will be the immensely rugged, super smart, and always empathetic elephants.

Picture Credits